For Expectant
Families

Angel
Within

By Othello Bach

Angel Within

For Expectant Families

To Margaret Sasser

my trusted friend and helper.

Little Light

When I first suspected your presence
I felt torn between tears of joy
and cries of fear.
What a wonderful blessing!
What an overwhelming responsibility!
Now, only sweet acceptance settles through me.
You are real. You are mine.
You are loved.

Sweet Presence

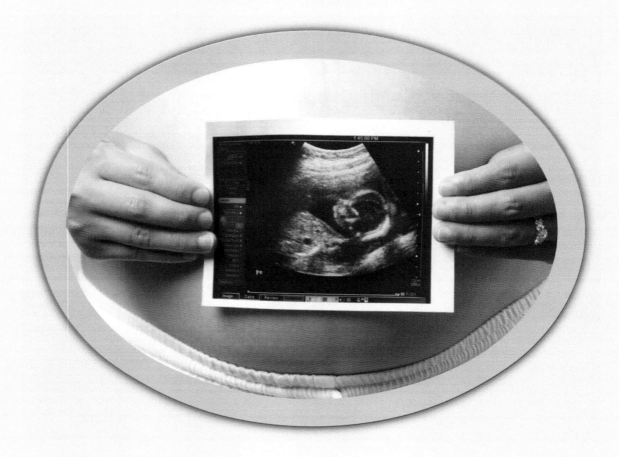

So powerful is your life!
Already, it has changed mine.
Since I first accepted you as real
I have thought of little else.
You have influenced every decision.
What could have made me worthy of this honor?
I'm sure I do not know.
But I give thanks because your life establishes a purpose
-an indisputable value-for my life.

Happy Thought

Heaven has extended Itself to me

And I have accepted!

We are One. So it is.

And so it always will be.

Growing Life

We grow together, little one,

in health, happiness,

and abundant love.

Together, we are changing,

and this change will benefit the world.

Remembered One

Often, when I go to bed at night,
I smile realizing I've thought of
nothing all day except you.

Even when I try to forget you
and think of something else...

you will not be forgotten!

What is this power you have... so
appealing... that each day ends
with a sense of quiet celebration?

Little Stranger

Sometimes I feel so frightened of you!

How can anything weighing only ounces

create such havoc when you're not even here!

Maybe it's not you that frightens me.

Maybe it's something that weighs nothing at all...

Maybe it's only a frightening thought.

How can a thought—something that weighs

nothing at all —feel so heavy?

Do you know the answer to that?

If you do... when you arrive... be sure to tell me.

Tiny Being

Last night your father sat for hours, and I know he was thinking of you. I could see into his mind, I think, and what I saw, I would like to share.

First, I saw love...love and pride so deeply felt, he had a radiance I had not seen before.

Then fear crept in, replacing the radiance with the look of one who's viewing himself in a mirror of distorted reflections - and doesn't know it.

For the longest while, I saw him considering all the questions: Can we do it? Can we love enough? Give enough? Care enough? Can we afford you?

Eventually, his struggle ended and an air of quietness settled over him. It was a peace and gentle reassurance, which I recognized because I have felt it, too.

At that moment, I knew he knew... We can do it. All of it.

You will be welcomed here with loving, open arms.

Little Love

Nothing can come between

God's love for me and you.

Brightest Star

We'll view the stars together. We'll try to count them all. They were made for you, and I suggest that every one hangs in its place just for your happiness.

Delightful One
The purest pleasure on earth
is the sound of a child's laughter.
You, my child, will laugh with joy and delight
at all the beauty life has to offer.

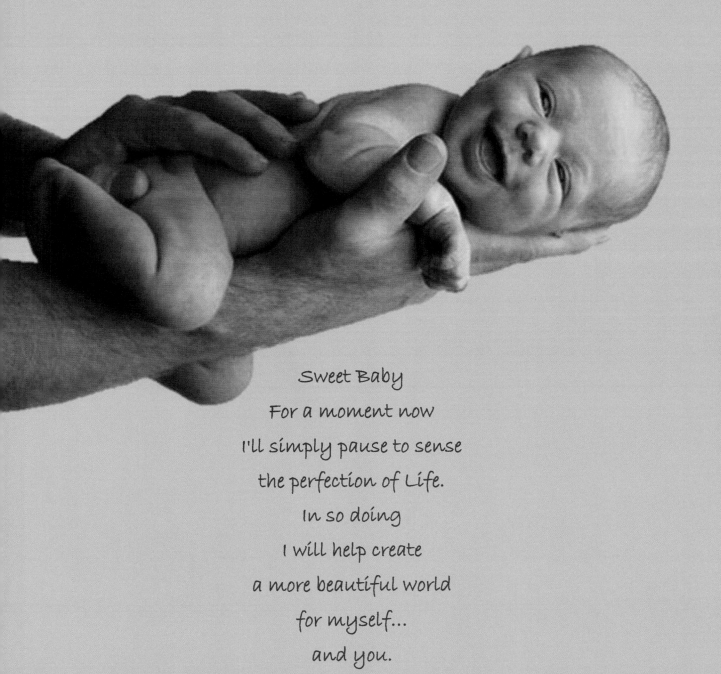

Sweet Baby

For a moment now

I'll simply pause to sense

the perfection of Life.

In so doing

I will help create

a more beautiful world

for myself...

and you.

Tiny Life
The Perfect Being Who created me
renews my faith in myself
so that I may believe
I am worthy of you.

Playful One

Will you like kittens?

Puppies? or frogs?

Oh, I know you'll like kittens

and puppies

because all children do.

If you like frogs

you'll have to play with them outside.

Precious One

No matter what the situation,
I will never lead you to believe
your father's love is less than mine.
Nor will I imply any lack
exists within him because
if you doubt him,
you will doubt yourself.

Greatest Sweetness

If all the beauty of the world
were pressed together
and made into a fragrant, rich perfume,
its sweetness would fade
next to the thought of you.

Special One

I turn within and awaken
to the Self that already knows
how to care for you.

Beautiful Being

I am aware that your
beautiful life has been given to me...
not to own, but to share and love.
I know who your True Creator is.

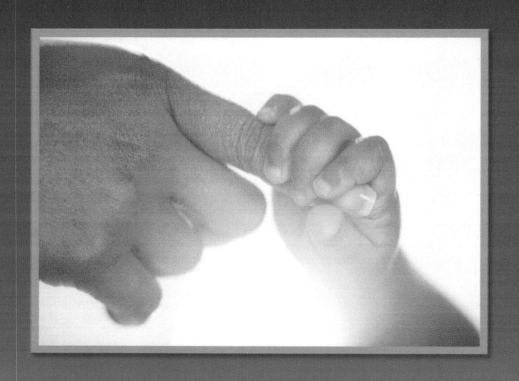

Impressionable One

The part I will play in your life
cannot be overstated.
The part God plays
cannot be exaggerated

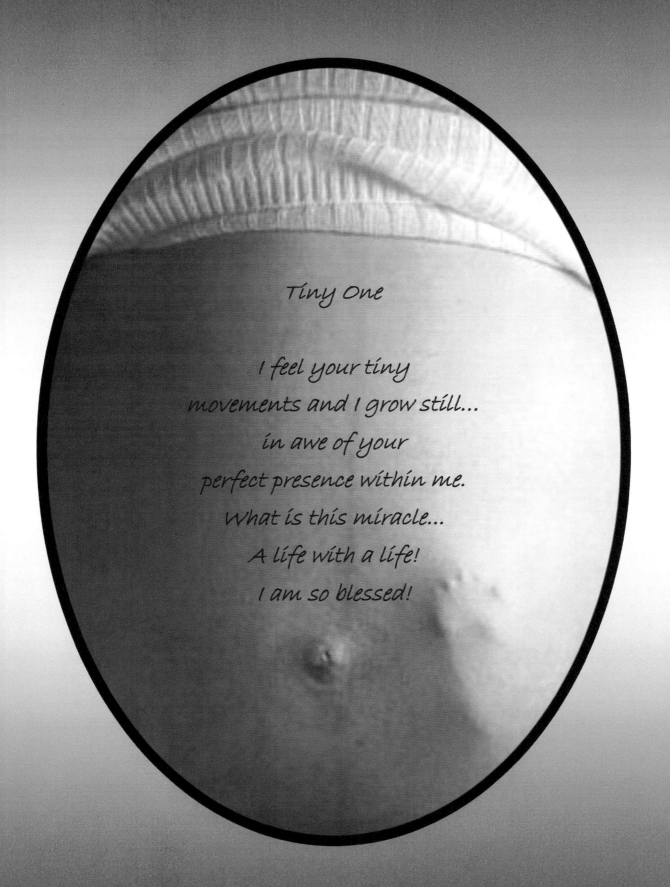

Tiny One

I feel your tiny
movements and I grow still...
in awe of your
perfect presence within me.
What is this miracle...
A life with a life!
I am so blessed!

Sweet Child

Peace fills my mind
and comforts my body
as I grow with you.

Comforting Being

I look inward
and listen to the Quiet Voice
which constantly assures me:
"All is well...Within and without."

Growing Awareness
My awareness expands
to include the ever-increasing
love which fills my life.

Beautiful Life

If you could see
through my eyes now,
you would see a rainbow arching high,
its beauty stretching through the air...
I'll keep its beauty in my mind for you to share.

Little Child

I will rise to meet the task
your life presents me.
You can count on this because
the strength we share comes from
a Power too great to fail us.

Little Spirit
I will not
let you forget
my love.

Sweet Inspiration

I will trust that the Power within you
is sufficient to inspire and defend you at all times.

This way, when I'm not with you,
I won't be afraid.
One tiny child...

One Great Spirit...
Wanting but one experience...
To love and be loved.
Already, this is so!

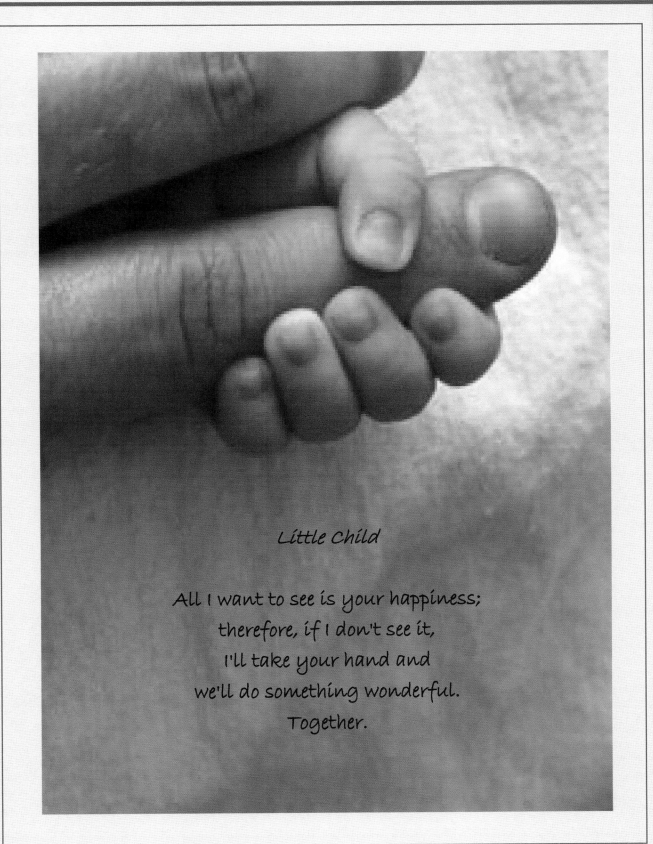

Little Child

All I want to see is your happiness;
therefore, if I don't see it,
I'll take your hand and
we'll do something wonderful.
Together.

Delightful Baby

Seeing what we love creates joy.
Seeing what we fear creates pain.
Therefore, I will look at every situation
until I see the happy, loving truth in it,
and only this will I share with you
...because I love you.

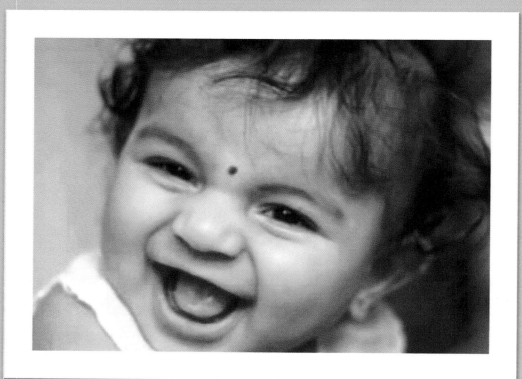

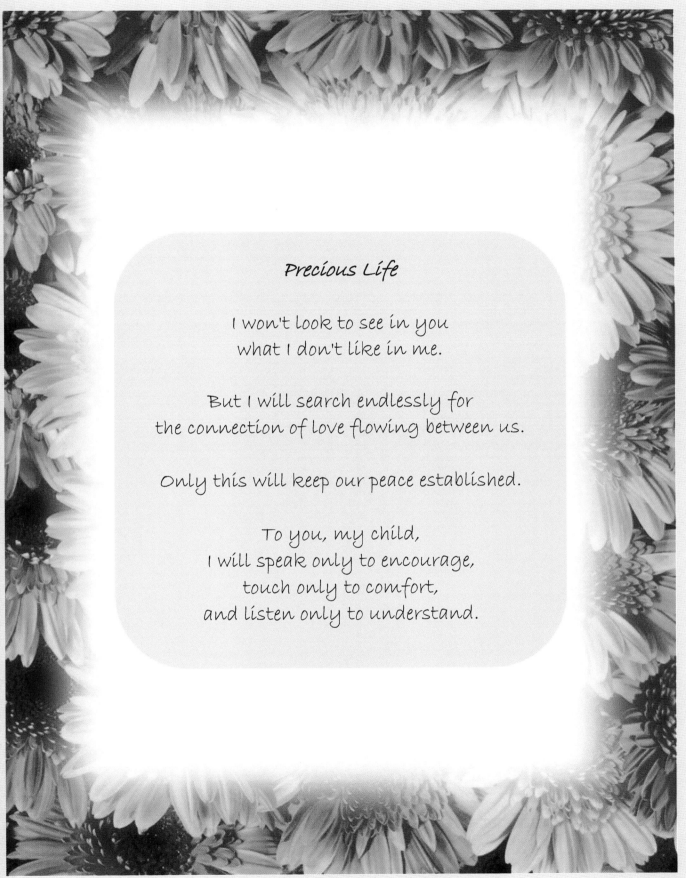

Precious Life

I won't look to see in you
what I don't like in me.

But I will search endlessly for
the connection of love flowing between us.

Only this will keep our peace established.

To you, my child,
I will speak only to encourage,
touch only to comfort,
and listen only to understand.

Sweet Child

I'll close my eyes to your mistakes
because mistakes are not important.
But your every kindness,
your every display of courage,
and your every accomplishment,
I'll repeat to everyone,
in your presence,
so you'll know I'm pleased with you.

Tiny One

I'll never hold you up to ridicule,
nor teach you to ridicule others
by doing so myself.
With your birth comes a new
and better life for me, too.

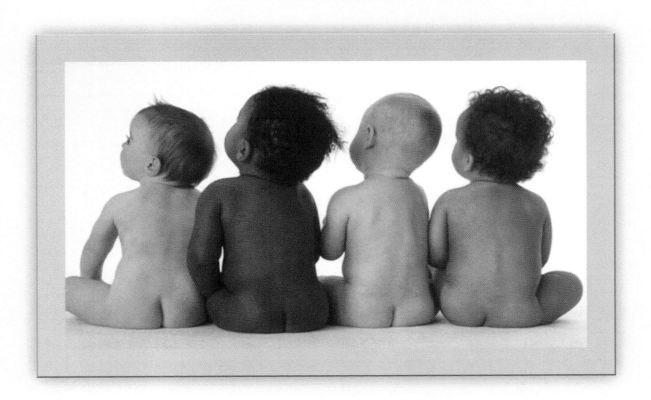

Important One

If I should think I'm not important,
your life will be evidence that I am.

Happy One

For you
I'll always have a smile.
Because of you
I'll always have reason to smile.

Impressionable Mind

What you fear will never be,
for what is feared is always in the future
and therefore, does not exist.
You are perfect,
whole and complete,
and neither your fears
nor mine can change that.

Perfect Child

I thank you because
I know you'll give me
joy greater than
I've ever known.

In waiting for you,
already you have done that!

Dear One

God has a way of stopping time
for those who want it stopped.

This, I'm sure I'll learn as you insist on
stopping to look at a bug,
pick up a stick, pat a dog,
or talk to a friend.

We who have been created in the image
and likeness of God have created you
—another image like Him—
to remind us that as we give,
we receive.

Child to Come

I promise to remember that
what I perceive as your shortcomings,
are merely beliefs I have mistakenly
accepted about myself and
projected onto you.

Remembering, I'll correct the problem
where it lives within myself.

Little Squirmer

Sometimes I lie awake at night
and feel you squirming, as you, like me,
try to find a comfortable position for the night.

Then we grow quiet, and I pray that you'll love us
as much as we love you.

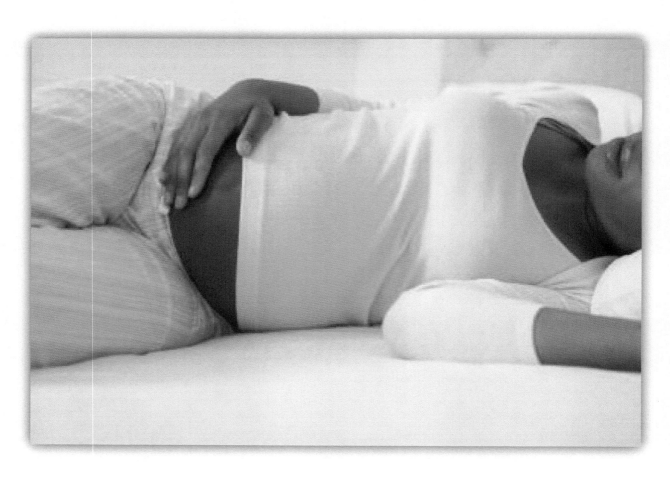

Welcomed Child

We speak of you often.
All of our plans include you now.
Your place is well established
in our home, in our minds,
and in our hearts.

Sweet One

Even when I'm in a hurry
and think I have no time to stop
and tell you that I love you...
I'll stop and tell you.

Active One

What is this commotion?
Will you be born already crawling?

After months of climbing up and down my ribs,
you've grown so strong!

Bless you, active child! And if you will...
please remove your boots before you're born.

Little Joy

As a child, I often felt guilty
because I thought my parents
were disappointed in me.

Remembering how awful that felt,
I want to assure you...
I know that only I can disappoint me.
You...yes you, are my joy!

You Who Can

Until you can, I'll do for you.
When you can, I'll observe
and encourage.

When you think you can't,
I'll remind you this is just a thought,
and let you prove you really can.

Unique Life

Let me resist the temptation
to mold you into another me.

Happy Child

Happiness is the greatest gift
you can give yourself.

Without it, you'll have nothing of value
to give others.

Sweet Being

I will do for you
as I would have you do for me
if our situations were reversed.

And if I find that "for some reason"
I am less than happy,
I'll remind myself I am the "reason"
and then I'll do for you
as you would do for me
if you knew how.

Child of Quality

Let me not forget that I did not create you alone.
Let me appreciate those qualities in you which I
do not recognize in myself.

Perhaps this way I, too, shall acquire them, and
a part of your beauty will become my own.

Precious Being

I am eager to learn
all you have to teach me.

Limitless Being

Anytime, Anywhere
You are free to be
anything you desire.

Expectant Spirit

You will come into my world expecting it to be beautiful, and I will never tell you it's not.

When the time comes
to deliver this beautiful being, I shall be calm because I go to do a noble thing.

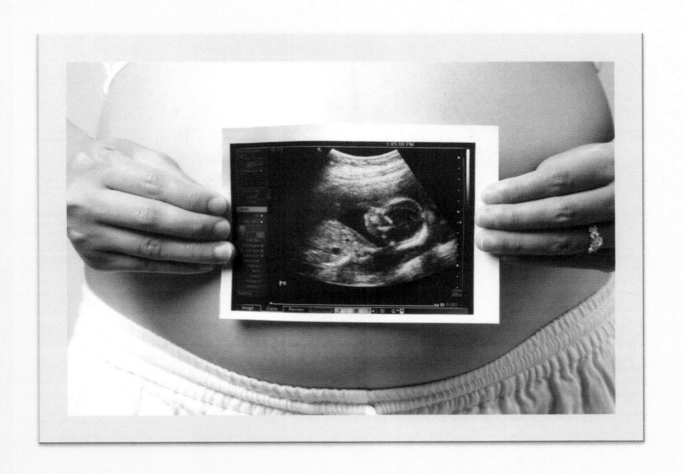

Crowding In

If you could see me now...
this thing that I've become...
you might have second thoughts about coming.

There are times when
"two being one"
isn't all it's cracked up to be.

Two beings crowded into
one is more like it.

Forgive Me

I see parents who seem to be careless.
I recall when I thought mine were, too.
I beg you, in advance, please forgive me for
the careless things I fear I'll do.

Growing Happiness

I pray that I'll not interfere with the Self you are directed to be.

I'll do my best to stand aside and let you grow strong and tall... not bent and leaning toward me, afraid to stand alone... not twisted and confused straining to grow around my stubborn, fixed beliefs.

I'll do my best to remember God has a reason for making you different from me.

What Will You Be?

Will you like to study or to daydream?

Will you like paints and glue or baseball bats and swings?

Judging from the cartwheels that you're turning,

I think you'll be a gymnast on the rings!

Bright Child

I will never tell you that your thinking is wrong. Instead, I will admire your creativity and help you find a more useful thought to think—one which will create the effect you're wanting to experience.

Driving Love

I wonder which of us feels more confined right now.
I feel you struggling to move and turn - but so am I.
You cannot hate the steering wheel more than I do.
And I would like for you to know...
If my legs were growing at the same rate as my stomach,
I would scoot the seat back!

But they're not.
So please be still. We'll be there soon.
(I hope!)

Precious One

The Light within you will never flicker nor grow dim, although you may forget it's there.

If you do, I'll share mine until yours shines bright again and you can see which way you want to go.

Innocent One

I'll not blame you for my unhappiness.

Little Spirit

When you're frightened, reach
out and take my hand.

I'll hold it out because you'll
have faith in me.

And your faith will give

me confidence enough to

steady you.

Lingering Love

The days grow long now as I wait for you. So anxious are my hours that
even the best company can't hold my attention.
Anytime, now.

Anytime.
I won't hurry you...
but oh! I'm anxious to see your face and my feet.

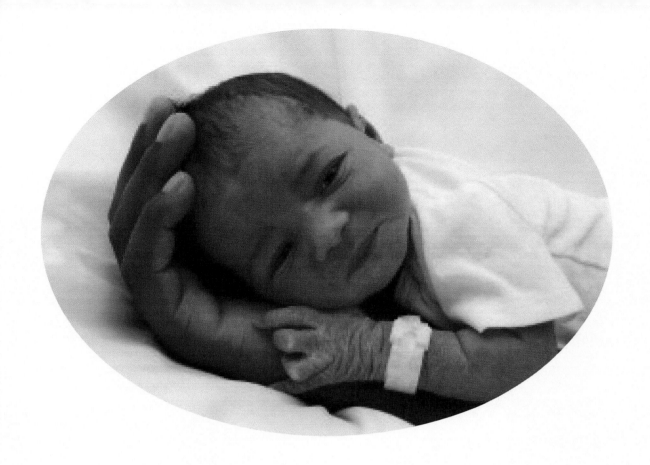

Patient Child

I know that as you grow we'll become different.

Some of what you'll like would not exist if it were up to me.

But because you'll be forced to be patient with my world,

the things you like I'll treat respectfully.

The only thought worth thinking is a happy one.

Courageous Child

I'll express my confidence in you
so you'll be confident.
If I doubt, I'll keep quiet,
so you can prove me wrong.

Child of Wisdom

You'll never have a problem that doesn't have at least two answers.

Choose the one that really makes you happy because that's the one that comes from God.

Special Child

Soon our special intimacy will be ended. The time is fast approaching when you'll break free to become your own unique and special self.

So much time has been spent in quiet projection of what you'll be like... I just have to ask:

Am I close? Have I come even a little close to knowing you? Breathlessly, I anticipate your arrival... another whole and perfect self.

Ready and Waiting

Your bed is ready, little one!
Your tiny things have all been washed, (more than
once, I must admit.)
I just couldn't resist... They're so tiny!

Yes, your bed is soft, but not as soft as the feeling in
our hearts. Last night I stood looking at your bed.
Oh, I long to hold you in my arms!

Tardy Child

Where are you?
I wait with something less than patience, now.
I sit, legs spread, upon my bed, like some
stranded, bloated cow.
All the prose and poetry have left me.

My swollen soul is stuck in this sore place.
Just limericks, which make me sick, like me,
they lack dignity and grace.

Angel in Disguise

I saw your face! I heard your cries!
Tiny angle hands... Perfect angel eyes.
The angel's face that I've longed to see
Through months of waiting impatiently.

At last, you appear, pretending to be
an ordinary infant but you can't fool me!
I recognize you! Don't you realize?
I can see... You're an angel in disguise!

Little Director

It's amazing that such a tiny hand can—without lifting a finger—lead me around and direct me to do exactly what it wants done.

Beloved Child

I know there will come a time when you
won't believe this...
but if you could see the love on your
father's face when he holds you...
you would always be the happiest, most
secure child in all the world.

Magic Squirt

I don't know how you do it!
How do you turn 16 ounces of milk into 36
ounces of water dribbled out in quarter-ounce
puddles leaked into 40 diapers-
sometimes less than 5 minutes apart?
When I am old and want a bed pan
—every hour on the hour—
remember what I did for you.

Crying Baby

Sometimes you cry and I smile because I'm rested

and want to comfort you.

Sometimes I'm tired and I cry, too.

Other times, you cry and cry and cry

and I panic because no matter how I try, I can't comfort you.

At these times, I hate myself!

I pick you up and pace the floor,

I put you down and pace some more.

I pick you up again, rock and coddle you,

and when you won't hush, I wring my hands in fear...

raise my voice... and frighten you.

Please, forgive me, little one,

but sometimes I just don't know what on earth to do!

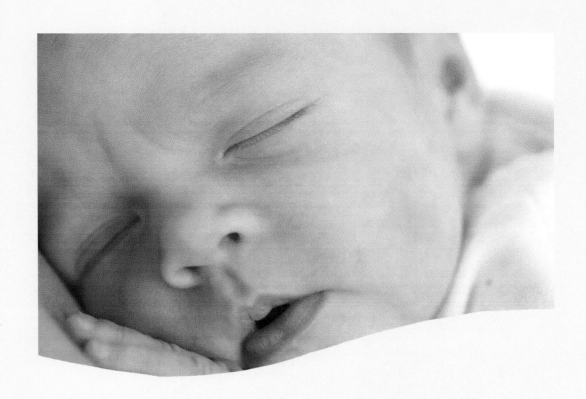

Good Morning, Little One

While we slept, the night's darkness
gave way to a bright morning sun.

We've been generously extended another
day in which to love each other.

Oh Beautiful Child

There are times when I can't take my eyes off you.

My love is so great and my pride so overwhelming,
nothing brings me greater satisfaction than to just
look at you and think quietly to myself:

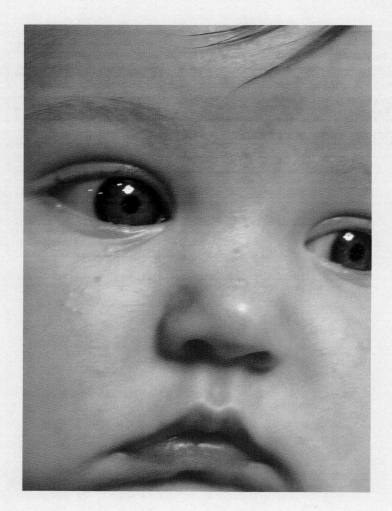

"This is my child! Isn't my child wonderful?"

Gentle Spirit

I see you squatting there, your eager
hands grasping for the cat (whose wary
apprehension I can see...)

I wonder how such a gentle spirit can
cause so much terror in the cat and me.

Each day I thank God for the
really important things like your
health, your happiness,
and disposable diapers.

Pride of My Life

The pride I feel in you sends my eyes
searching the faces of those around
me to see if they admire you as much
as you deserve to be admired.

The smart ones do.

Little Clutter-Up

Why do I bother to clean house?

It's clear you have no appreciation for the
fine art of neatness. You like the kitchen best when all the
pots and pans block my entry and cereal has been
dumped from wall to wall.

Although you're still in diapers,
I think I can safely predict you'll never be
hampered by excessive compulsions
to clean and tidy up.

This is good. The money you'll save on
psychologists can be spent to hire a maid.

Happy Hummer

You hummed! I heard you humming!
As I watched you play all absorbed in toys and
daydreams, I'm sure I heard you hum!

But when I crouched beside you, you stopped
humming and laughed at me for listening when
you weren't humming anymore.

Your sense of humor seems a little warped.

Sleeping Doll

When I watch you sleep, I'm sure that
the sweetness that rushes through me
is the love behind all life.

Rough and Tumble

Held by strong, loving arms you fly about the room
streaming drool and giggles through the air as your
father plays his rough and tumble games.

He calls it "airplane."

I call it insane.

I think God knew strong arms would be wasted on a
woman who would never see a need to lift a child
higher than her breasts.

"Mama!"

At home, In the car,

In the market, In the park

It doesn't matter where — I forget my name.

Is it instinct, this eagerness to hear you?

Even when you're miles away I answer

any child who calls, "Mama!"

I'm sure I used to have another name.

Protected Love

Last night the darkness parted for a
moment and I saw you... grown... filled with
confidence and grace.

And I knew that all the fearful things I'm
tempted to believe have no basis in reality.

You are here... so am I.

We are here... so is God.

Where God is, what could there be to fear?

Little Person...

I think one of the most confusing
situations in the world is that my
mother-in-law is also your grandmother.

How can the most intimidating person in
my life be the most adoring person in
yours?

It's hard to dislike someone who loves you so
much. I'm not sure I like being forced into
forgiveness this way.

Expressions of Love

Your father watches you play and tiny lines of happiness crinkle the corners of his eyes. He watches you cry and tries to comfort you, and tiny lines of sadness hold his mouth firmly fixed in discontent.

He cares... he loves you so deeply. Yes, this man loves you with a passion almost too great to be expressed.

Sleepy Baby

Because you sleep so peacefully
I know that someone more
observant than I is
watching over you.

Thank God for that.

Your Precious Smile

When I see you smile, a strange and wonderful gladness
makes me smile, too.

Could it be that the bond of life and love which runs between us
connects our smiles and tears
because we are one?

I hope so.

Constant Mess

When will you get it?

Eat in the high chair.
Potty in the potty chair.
Maybe if I get another high chair and
cut the bottom out...

It was easier to train the dog.

My Responsibility

There are still times when the
responsibility for overseeing your life
leaves me weak and breathless.

If I dwell on it, I doubt myself, and
resent the enormity of it all.

Then, before my fear can overcome me,
you toddle in to ask some
simple question:

"Can we plant some birdseed and
grow some birds?"

I realize then that I have only small,
joyful tasks to perform.

The complex tasks belong to God.

Guided Child

Your path is clear.
You know your way.

The key to happiness and
health is within you.

God, Himself, placed it there

so you would never lose it.

Child of Destiny

There is a purpose for your life that's so sure and certain the
sun will leave its course before it would be left unknown to
you.

You will know it by the happiness it brings! It is the thing
that when you do it both time and space disappear,
and when it's completed your
energy is greater than when you began.

Walk calmly then and speak with the authority of one who
knows that each life has a divine purpose.

Child of Mine

No matter where you go, who you're with,
what you're doing or how old you are, I will
always be thinking of you, praying for you,
and loving you with all my heart.

Because I am your mother.

NOW

Someday, because I love you I'll let you go.

Sometimes, because you love me,
you'll come visit me.

Now because we're together, let's not
worry about someday and sometimes...
let's enjoy the time we have!

Othello is a multi-genre author of numerous books which range in scope and variety from suspense novels to children's books to non-fiction "How-to" books. Her memoir "Cry into the Wind," chronicles an abusive childhood, including 11 years in an orphanage. Although a non-reader until the eighth grade, she wrote and sold her first novel to Avon Books when she was 22.

Othello often composes music and lyrics to accompany her children's stories, and celebrities Joel Grey, Tammy Grimes and Sandy Duncan have recorded her books and songs. She is a motivational speaker who loves to share "the tools" that helped her overcome an abusive past.

Othello welcomes all reader questions and comments, email her at othellobach@comcast.net

www.amazon.com/author/othellobach

www.othellobach.com

www.whoeverheardofafird.com

Other Books by Othello Bach
*not yet available in eBook format

Fiction
Simon Sees
Tainted
House of Secrets*
Satan's Daughters
Rail Fever*
Trapped
Brimstone Brethren*
The Sacrifice
The Taking of Joanna*

Nonfiction
Cry Into the Wind
How to Write a Great Story
Life After Trauma and Abuse*
Body Designing
101 Questions for God
The Father Within
Grow Your Self
Secrets of Successful Writers

Children's
Albert and the Monster
Whoever Heard of a Fird
Snigglefuzzle
Does My Room Come Alive at Night
Hector McSnector and the Mail Christmas Order Witch*
Jake Snake's Race
Lilly, Willy and the Mail Order Witch*
Monica's Hanukkah House*
Snyder Spider's Birthday Surprise*
The Biggest Sneeze
The Man With Big Ears
Golden Slippers